*"Dreams are free. Goals have a cost.
While you can daydream for free, goals don't come
without a price. Time, Effort, Sacrifice, and Sweat.
How will you pay for your goals?"*

Usain Bolt

Explore Neuroscience of Self-Discipline for Life Improvement

A Practical Guide to Love Yourself, Control Feelings and Emotions, Build Good Habits and Develop a Focused Mind

Ray G. Clear

—

Contents

—

Introduction

At any given time, there's likely a cell phone around you. With this handheld device, you can search for anything at any time, so long as you have service.

Now think about the large organ behind your eyes and in between your two ears. Having the technology of our cellphones at our fingertips seems incredible, but we often forget about the one thing powering our lives: our brain.

Your cellphone likely has between 32-128 GB of available storage, though many go much further than this.
Your brain can hold anywhere from 10,000 to 100,000 GB of information. Some experts believe we could even hold as many as 2,500,000 terabytes.
Imagine how expensive phone like that would be!

Neuroscience dives into the biology of the nervous system. This involves everything from your sensory perception to your thoughts.
With such a broad topic, there's a lot to unpack.

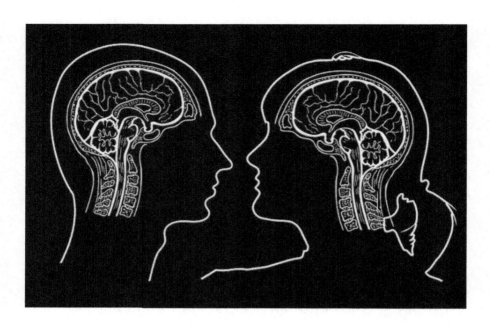

One aspect most of us should pay more attention to is the neuroscience of our self-control.

Lacking self-control can affect your health by causing you to ignore your nutrition, avoid exercise, fail to find success at work, stress out over easy things, and ignore your desire to learn more.

Everything we do can connect back to an impulse, which can lead to specific behaviors. In life, most of us strive to act in a way that enhances all aspects of our lived experiences in many different areas.

Unfortunately, our own mind can be the one thing keeping us from this happiness.
If you struggle with self-love, controlling your emotions, stopping bad habits, or maintaining concentration, you are likely struggling in more areas than one. You are not alone in this process.

As we have already covered, the brain is pretty complex! It is a very understudied area, partially because there is so much we have yet to understand.

By cultivating self-discipline, strengthening willpower, creating healthier habits, and controlling your emotions, you can improve your life, no matter which area is lacking.

The barrier to any change is a lack of willpower. That desire, motivation, and longing for something greater are required to propel you into success.
No one else is going to provide this for you.
The absence of an internal stimulus can leave us feeling lost, hopeless, and struggling with our identity. Too often people depend on external stimuli for their motivation. They let society tell them what career to pick, how to dress, and even what movies to watch or music to listen to.
The desire and strength need to be uncovered from within. It's not something that's always easily found, and it won't be obvious. Sometimes you have to go through tough things to see it, but when you actively take the chance to seek that deeper motivation, it gives you a basis to be more willful. When you have something to fight for, it's easier to throw the first punch.

Now is the time to get up and go! No one is going to hand you your life because most will be concerned with finding their own.
Your self-discipline does not run out. You don't have a meter for your willpower, despite what some might have believed in the past.
Are you ready to begin this change? It all starts by diving deep into what it means to have willpower in the first place.

CHAPTER 1

Neuroscience of Self-Discipline, the Engine of Success

If the barrier to success is a lack of self-discipline, then it's easy to see that the engine towards your most significant achievement is through strong willpower.

On a secondary level, you might think of self-discipline as your ability to not commit a crime, to get up in the morning and go to work, and to resist eating the entire bag of chips. In some ways, that is true, but it is so much more than that.
Self-discipline involves saying 'no,' to that second slice of pizza, resisting the urge to call in sick in the morning just because you don't want to go to work, and your ability not to do anything illegal.
These are more natural ways to understand self-control, but there are more complex motives and effects on a deeper level.

It involves having the strength to love yourself and turn away when you start to be your biggest bully. It's the ability to say, "Hey, that's not true," when you tell yourself you're not worthy. You can refocus your energy on what you can do going forward rather than what you should have done in the past. It's your power to confront bad habits and create new ones. It's your method of staying more focused on the things that require your attention.

Impulse control lies within the prefrontal cortex. There is where you make judgments, manage aggression, reason, and control your emotions as well. This impulse is a reminder that your willpower involves your perception and emotions more than you might think on the surface. Sometimes our urges feel almost animalistic, but they are much more logical than you might think.

Willpower and Self-Discipline

What is *willpower*?

What does it mean to have *self-discipline*?

To begin, you can look at some of the most inspirational people of our time. Men and women of sports, actors, politicians, and other successful individuals can show us what it means to practice a little self-restraint.

Usain Bolt became one of the fastest men on the planet by focusing on nothing but sports. His discipline came from his passion, knowing nothing else other than the competitions as he practiced from his rural Jamaican hometown.
Keanu Reeves has experienced more grief and loss than most, and yet he's still managed to become one of the highest-paid actors of our time.
Winston Churchill led the United Kingdom through one of the worst wars in history; environmental activist Greta Thunberg has been a face to a global movement targeting climate change, and Michelle Obama continues to empower women across the planet with her wise words.

What is one thing that all of these people have in common?
Do they sit around and watch TV?
Do they enjoy activities that others might see as timewasters?

Winston Churchill

They likely do it at some point, but with all other activities, they also practice a high level of self-control.

High willpower involves constraining oneself against impulse. Self-control is a little more mental but still involves blocking yourself from giving in to the most significant impulses that present themselves to you.

Impulses come in all shapes and sizes.
What impulses come to your mind?
The impulse to eat a second bowl of ice cream?
The impulse to wait until Sunday night to study?
The impulse to skip the gym, the instinct to cheat on your partner, hurt somebody else, hurt yourself?

Impulses are simple and ordinary, like watching one more episode even though you should have gone to bed an hour ago.
Impulses are also extreme, like wanting to punch someone in the face when you're upset.

Self-control is the tool we use to combat these significant impulses. Self-control involves looking inward and recognizing what urge these impulses are telling you needs to be fulfilled.
When you hear your stomach rumble, you eat. When you feel your stomach hurt, you go to the bathroom. These are normal and healthy acts based on impulses we have.
When you're stressed out, you might reach for the liquor cabinet. When you're feeling angry, you might lash out on a friend.

Some impulses might seem out of our control but are still in the domain of what we have power over.
It's easy to cast blame elsewhere when we struggle with our impulse.
How many times have you heard someone say, "I can't help it, I was mad!"?

The thing about our willpower is that it is malleable. We can increase, decrease, strengthen, and weaken it. It is not finite, and there isn't a limit to how many things you could say 'yes' or 'no' to.

In the remainder of this book, we will go straight to the point of how you can play with this malleability.

Having self-control isn't about creating a strict or stagnant mindset. Don't think of self-control as locking yourself away from life's joys. Instead, understand that you already exist in a mental prison in which your impulses are your unruly guards.

Imagine being on a restricted diet. Think of having to go on a diet. Having to turn down candy or ice cream doesn't seem like fun to most.
What kind of happy life is one filled with so much restraint? However, the real control comes from those sweets. If you can't say 'no' comfortably to your impulses, you don't have control over them—they have the power over you.
Willpower isn't about punishing your mind. It's all about taking back control from the impulses that have led you so far astray in the first place.

Mindfulness Will Award You

Your thoughts are endless.
On any given day, you could have anywhere from 40,000 thoughts up to about double that on average. It's impossible to track your thoughts. Sometimes they are complex, letting you question your reality or perspective. Other times they're as simple as "What's that smell?"

These thoughts can leave us feeling drained, worried, and defeated daily.
Something as simple as a nasty glimpse from a coworker can have you questioning every last move you make throughout the day.

Mindfulness is a way to pull you from the endless thoughts you are having. Whether you are repetitively thinking of your biggest regrets, or you're going over the worst possible consequence of a situation, mindfulness can pull you from these patterns and place you back in a more grounded area, helping to have a healthier outlook on life.

To be mindful, notice everything is surrounding you. Become aware of who you are and where you are standing. Notice everything from the way you physically feel to the thoughts passing through your mind.

Do your best to focus on physical objects. You can do this by assigning yourself what to look out for, observing a specific color or counting objects in front of you.

Right now, look around you and pick out everything is gray. Don't overthink it, and if you miss something, that's fine. It's not a game or competition. It's merely a way to lock your focus into the present.

Meditation is a more advanced version of this. To begin meditating, you have to commit at least five minutes a day to clear out your mind. Some people will only be able to focus for 30 seconds at a time when they first start meditation, but with the right practice, you can grow that into an hour or even more. Meditation involves focusing on your breathing and pushing all thoughts out of your mind as they occur.

Both mindfulness and meditation rewire your brain because they keep you from diving into unnecessary rumination. You're training yourself to be more aware. Often we let our thoughts run wild without ever gaining hold of them. Instead of reflecting and asking, *"Why am I thinking this, and how is this thought affecting my life?"* Many individuals will let themselves be driven on impulse, trying to satisfy one thought to the next.

With tens of thousands of thoughts passing through our minds daily, it's impossible to give in to every demand. Instead, we have to know how to let most of these thoughts pass, focusing only on the most important ones.

This prioritization changes your attitude because the next time an issue appears, you're less likely to lash out and more likely to be calm and collected with your responses. Instead of associating a stressful moment with a trigger to lash out, you'll be able to stay focused on what you need to.
The key to self-discipline is reflection. If you can't notice and identify your thoughts, you can't dispute them in and control them.

Becoming mindful is the first step. To get deeper into meditation, check out easy guides through YouTube videos or audiobooks to help keep you grounded in today.

Self-Control Practices

One of the most effective ways to increase your self-discipline and willpower is to keep a journal. Daily writing your activities will force you to ponder and be accountable for your self-reflection correctly.
Every day you can have periods of reflection. You can schedule it just for ten minutes before going to bed, or it could be as long as an hour ordeal if you like.
Journaling doesn't have to be a creative process.
Some people enjoy writing poetry, stories, or even doodling as a way to reflect.

You might be more analytical and enjoy using numbers. You can do that in your way!
A straightforward method is to record your thoughts or actions throughout your day.
You can create a chart to keep track of what you are doing consistently.

For example, you might tally all the times you are hard on yourself. You can make a quick note for each time you get distracted by checking your phone. You could record all the moments you give into food impulses.
At the end of the week, you can gather your daily recordings and enter them into a graph to have a more rational way to evaluate your thoughts and behaviors.
Once you have accumulated all the right information and begun this essential reflection process, then you can begin to lead yourself.

The first way to achieve results is to know what is in and out of your control.
Often, we try to change things that are out of our control and give others the power over things we do hold the reins to.
You have no control over some aspects, like the thoughts and opinions of others or even your background.
You could change your hair, your eye color (contact lenses), and even your skin color (tanning/bleaching), but you can't change where you have come from or your past life.
You can influence someone's opinion or inspire them to think a certain way, but ultimately it is the individual mind that is in control of their beliefs.

You have some control over certain circumstances. For instance, you could quit your job, but you still have to find a way to pay your bills. Or you could just change your job, but you still have to find a position within your abilities.

You have complete control over your decisions and your emotions.
Again, others could influence or inspire these feelings, but it is you that has the last word on your emotions.
You need to understand the importance of external thoughts and how they affect your behavior.

Everything starts with a stimulus, a trigger, or a cause.
Next will usually come to a reaction, which might be anger, disgust, shock or frustration.
Afterwards is the response, how you decide to react like crying, punching, or laughing.

Your control lies between your reaction and your response.
We can't control the cause every time, but what comes after does lie within our power.

For example, let's go through this cycle of **cause – reaction – response**.

Let's say the case is a thunderstorm on your wedding day.
The reaction is a probable disappointment; it could be frustration, stress, or a combination of all three.
The response is where your choice lies. You could cancel the wedding. You could scream at the venue staff. You could cry while you sit in the rain and eat your wedding cake with your bare hands.
You could also laugh it off and move everything inside. You could say, "*Water isn't going to hurt anyone*" and get married in the rain! These conditions are all under your control. You might think, "*I can't help it if I cry or laugh*" It is right in some situations.

That stimulus might be so intense it does give those visceral reactions. A person who cries all the time isn't necessarily a person who has no control over their emotions. The principal distinction you have here is your view on the action of crying. Someone who embraces their tears and cries freely might have a lot more control over someone who thinks crying is weak and always hides their emotions. On some level then, we have to recognize this is still within our control.
Another practice you can do is to know what your strengths and weaknesses are.
What is it that you would like to improve? For this practice, your journal will come very handy.

List your weaknesses. For each one that you have, identify a strength. Then, go back to the weaknesses and decide if they need to be eliminated, adjusted, or embraced.

For example, a weakness might be that you always give in to your cravings. This likely needs to be eliminated.

Another weakness might be that you have too much empathy and always say 'Yes' when people ask for help. This could be adjusted, and you still can say 'Yes' but also be focused on saying 'No' in times that you need to take care of yourself.
A weakness might be that you get so stressed about planning a trip that you feel overwhelmed. In this case, the preparation can be contained, and emotional management enhanced.

Start to practice your thoughts; you can simply do it in your mind.
When riding the train or on the bus, look outside the window and reflect; avoid staying all-time reading or scrolling through your phone.
Have conversations with yourself.
Don't' just let your thoughts glide by, but instead question them as if two people are discussing your brain.
If you think to yourself,
"I'm hideous; I need to do something to change"
respond with
"I don't know if that's true. Who told me that I am ugly? Why do I believe this?"

Write your thoughts down to give them more emphasis. Sometimes as you write them, you'll discover how ridiculous they are, making it easier to overcome them.

Unravel your thinking to make connections about how your opinions are affecting your behavior.
This is a common practice in cognitive behavioral therapy.
Trace the issue back to the source, is this a thought that developed in your childhood? Was it planted there by a parent, teacher, or bully? Did you pick it up from society, or is it just a product of other thoughts you've had?
These are the beginning practices to help you tap into the neuroscience of your brain. The further you explore, the more secrets to your mind you'll unlock.

Strengthen Willpower to Redesign Your Life

Once you become aware of your thoughts, it's hard to stop. The deeper you dive into your mind, the closer you get to unlocking who you are.
What we discussed so far are more mental processes. Once you start to tap into that surface level of neuroplasticity, you can begin to get deeper into behavioral practices that change the way you think as well.

As we already mentioned, journaling is a beneficial and healthful way to reflect, as is analytically tracking your day.
One journaling exercise you can do is to write letters to your past self, and - why not - to other people as well.
Let your feelings pour onto the page, and don't cut yourself off. Say anything and everything you want to say. Tell your past self why you are so angry. Tell your friend you're mad at them. Tell your mom you resent her. Do whatever you have to get your emotions out.
Once you are done, look it over. Often what happens is you discover a lot of these things aren't actually what you feel. Sometimes they're just thoughts that pass by, and we let our minds believe to be true.
When you are satisfied with the letters, destroy them. This action is particularly crucial if you wrote an angry letter to someone and hope they don't see it!

A different way to strengthen willpower is by focusing on eating a healthier and more balanced diet.

Your brain runs off glucose.

It needs carbohydrates for energy. When you provide it with empty carbs all day long, like white bread, pasta, sugars, and so on, this doesn't give your brain all the energy needed. Instead, more complex elements are required, like whole wheat and natural sugars found in fruits and vegetables. Additives, like preservatives, flavor enhancers, and food dyes, can also dramatically affect your brain.

To increase self-control, it sometimes involves checking in with biological factors such as your diet.

Another healthy neuroscience practice is to switch things around physically, whether it's in your home or office.

When you materially change a space, it's easier to rearrange mentally as well. We get so used to specific settings that our brains can go on autopilot. It's easy to keep falling into the same habits when you keep putting yourself in the same place. So, move the furniture or paint the walls, hang a new picture and add some houseplants for the better of the change.

Positive affirmations are also helpful for creating better self-discipline.

Telling yourself, "*I can't do this*", "*I shouldn't even bother*" or "*Nothing matters*" can often leave you lacking motivation. Turn these into the opposite phrase to give you more inspiration, like, "*I can do this*", "*I am strong*" or "*I matter*".

Write them down, put them on your wall, and repeat them to yourself as often as possible to replace the negative thoughts with the new.

Give at least an hour of your time a week to reflect and improve your brain's willpower.
You could give yourself 20 minutes every day to reflect, or you could just do an hour every Sunday to write in your journal.
It's essential to dedicate yourself to and schedule these times to ensure you are keeping up with your mental health.

CHAPTER 2

Key Factors to Activate Self-Discipline

At the moment, one of the most significant problems in your process is likely to be stress.
Stress is natural and normal, and it's never going away. The problem is not that you have anxiety, but that you don't have the self-control to manage it.

Stress can be a motivator. It is what motivates you to go to work and pay bills or to go to the gym to avoid heart disease.
However, motivation also needs to be found in something good, which can be discovered on a journey of self-discovery.
To achieve this, you can use a growth mindset to develop what you already know continually and to dive deeper into the remainder of the unknown.

Of course, to accomplish any goal, you have to make sure to take care of your body both physically and mentally, including having a good quality of sleep.
Your health is the most important thing you have, and a significant factor in how you care for that is found in how you experience and manage stress.
Too much pressure can shrink your prefrontal cortex. The more stressed you are, the easier it is to change the shape of your brain and often in the wrong way.

Stress Reduces Willpower

Stress is a chemical reaction that occurs in your body. Each time your body senses a warning, it will release a chemical known as cortisol.
This helps your body prepare for defense by raising your heart rate, increasing your breathing, tensing your muscles, and sharpening your focus.

In times when we used to have threats like lions, tigers and bears lurking around, this was necessary to alert us to either fight the hazard off or run away.

Stress affects your mind in many different ways.
We live a much cushier life behind our office desk than in the wild fields facing sharp-toothed predators.
However, the stress is still there. Instead of being scared of being eaten alive by a leopard, you're scared about how you're going to pay your mortgage, getting the right number of social media followers, or even picking out a movie to watch later.
It makes you more anxious.
Stress can leave us ruminating over the "what ifs" to the point that we stress ourselves even more, and it can increase impulsive behavior.

Your brain senses danger and wants immediate relief. This is known as the fight or flight response.

If you are stressed about paying your bills, you can fight this urge by working hard to make money, or you could act impulsively and alleviate those feelings by getting drunk and forgetting about your problems for the night.

Being too stressed makes it harder to have a positive outlook on life.

Sometimes we don't have an immediate solution so our brains will travel everywhere else in an attempt to find one. Often this just leaves us feeling more stressed than we did at the origin.

The physical effects of stress are hard on your body. Continually straining your muscles can lead to a sore back or neck; you might get a stomachache from the disruption of your hormones after the release of cortisol. Or you might feel like you can't breathe after your respiration and heart rate increased rapidly, maybe even leading to a panic attack.

Acting on impulse is only temporary relief.
To truly feel better in the long term, you need to get
to the root of the problem.
You can do it through the self-reflection processes
discussed in the previous chapter.
Often, understanding who we truly are - including our
motivations - can help us to find the real relief rather
than passing attempts at alleviation.

What Really Motivates You?

Overcoming impulse and increasing willpower involve
knowing better oneself.
It is essential to understand what you are doing, why
it is wrong, and why you want to improve.
What is waiting for you at the end of this journey of
self-discovery? If you have the motivation, it's easier
to have self-control.
Understand that life is a journey, not just a quick trip.
Stop waiting until later to be happy, that's the exact
issue with willpower.
We think life starts once we hit high school. Then this
idea ends, and we believe our new life will begin when
we're in college; at university, we'll be thinking life
starts as soon as we find a partner.
After that, we'll be waiting to build our career for a
new life starts; then it happens once we have kids, the
house, the car, etc.

Life doesn't wait around.
It's what is already happening and what we are living.
You don't have to wait until you achieve all your goals
to be happy. The journey is your life, full of fun and
rewards along the way.

Start asking yourself the hard questions to get closer
to understanding your motivation, such as:

• Who is most important to you?

• What is most important to get in life?

• What would you never regret doing if you found out
you were dying tomorrow?

• What do you fear you will continue to do the most?

• Would your present self-disappoint your past
person?

There are two different types of people who don't know themselves — those that don't even bother, and those that overthink it.
You have to find yourself somewhere in the middle. Questioning too much makes you talk yourself out of things.
If you are diving too deep in your thoughts or continually asking the 'why' of all aspects, it can generate even more doubt.

The key is having intention – knowing what you are reflecting for and what you are hoping to gain.
It is essential to have a clear target to scope at the end of your journey, but you also need to hold something extraordinary in your life now.

Grow the Mindset to Activate Discipline

There are many underlying beliefs that people have about learning, which can keep them trapped in a toxic mentality.
These beliefs retain people in the same mindset over and over again, preventing them from learning anything valuable.
One theory is that learning is academic and only done in a school setting; other false beliefs include:

- The older you are, the smarter you are

- Learning is only necessary for your job

- You can't keep learning past a certain age

- There's only so much you can know

The idea that anyone is more or less intelligent than someone else can also be a negative mentality.
Intelligence is not measured by just what you know.
There are many different types of brilliance.
You could know everything about space but be utterly clueless at managing your emotions.
You could be the most stoic, emotionally managed person, but not know how to boil water.
Intelligence is not measured. Instead, it is like a plant. Sure, one plant might be bigger than another, but that doesn't mean it's healthier.
Your brain is like a seed. It's grown into a plant throughout your life but going forward it's time to let it grow bigger. Keep changing the pot, fertilizing it, trimming it, and maintaining it not just to keep it alive, but to watch it flourish.
A growth mindset is all about how people learn.
Self-discipline is more influential in those with a growth mindset because they're better at analyzing and learning.
If you have a growth mindset, you won't make assumptions or jump to conclusions; rather than acting on impulse, you force yourself to question if something is good or bad for you.

To become more disciplined, allow your mind to grow.

Quality Sleep Will Boost Your Energy

Just like stress, rest is a chemical process. Not getting the right amount of sleep could mean a disruption in your hormones.
Lacking quality sleep can have many adverse side effects, such as:

• Feeling hungrier, leading to unhealthy decisions

• Limiting your ability to pay attention and focus

• Higher body weight because of the hormonal imbalance or food cravings

• Mood swings

• Increased stress, depression, and anxiety

• Higher risk of stroke or heart attack

On the most basic level, it slows you down from the lack of so much energy.
Being tired can have the same effect as being stressed out, and both will influence one another.
You might be stressed out because you are so tired, but at night, you are too stressed to sleep.
It's a vicious cycle that can only be stopped once we have given ourselves a restful night's sleep.
The first step towards better sleep is noticing the actions that are preventing you from getting that sleep in the first place; this could be anything from having a caffeinated soda before bed to sleeping with the TV on all night.

Make sure that you stick to the same sleep schedule nightly. Your body will get into a natural routine so by not doing this, you are depriving your biological structure the chance to regulate this hormonal balance.

Don't sleep with any lights on whatsoever. If you are afraid of the dark and have trouble sleeping when it is pitch-black, try getting a night light specifically made to mimic natural light, like the glow from the moon. Don't keep your phone anywhere near your bed. Put it across the room to not only ensure you aren't checking messages all night but so you have to physically get up out of bed to turn any alarms off, making it harder to hit the snooze button.
Only set one alarm per morning. By waking up every five minutes, you're just making it harder to get up out of bed that final time. The more care you put towards your sleep patterns, the easier it is to boost other aspects of your health.

Move Your Body to Generate Commitment

Exercise is essential because it is all about balancing your body.
Often it is associated with your physical appearance, but it's crucial for most internal functions too.
Oxygen is necessary for your brain to operate, and exercise increases the blood flow to your brain.

There are many other benefits of exercise, such as:

- Hormone regulation
- Stronger synapse connections
- Mindful awareness
- Boost in serotonin
- Memory enhancement
- Stress reduction

We all need 150 minutes of training in a week. It means about 20 minutes a day, but you can pick and choose when and how frequently you exercise. Spread out the activity time over the week is best, but if you want to knock it out all at once in 150 minutes, no one is stopping you.
Cardio is best for most people but remember to include some strength training to mix it up.

Most of us know we need to exercise more, but the problem is knowing how to do it better.
First, identify what triggers might be keeping you from exercising.
Are you afraid of judgment from people at the gym?
Do you only not like being sweaty?

Just as you address other negative thoughts, you have to come up with a method to confront and overcome these triggers.
Look at exercise in a completely new way; forget what you've known about it before.
You don't have to associate it with athleticism; exercising can also be very creative. Think of yoga or dance. Alternatively, you can be more practical with it, like self-defense through karate or boxing.

The most important thing to remember is to avoid the way of practice that let you fail before.
If you are always going to the same gym, but time after time you eventually stop, find a new gym.
If you have an exercise bike sitting in the corner of your room covered in clothes, trade it in for new equipment, or just move it and exercise elsewhere.

It's hard to create new habits by repeating the same old patterns!

Focus on aerobic exercises to stimulate brain health through higher production of oxygen.

These include:

swimming
running
biking
jogging
dancing
kickboxing
skiing

Start small. Something is always better than not exercising at all.
Even if you do ten minutes a day for a week, you can try to do twenty minutes a day the next, or also double it.
Change up your routine throughout the week to ensure you're not getting sick of doing the same thing over and over again.
Find unique ways to bring exercise into what you are already doing, making it a more natural part of your life.
The change can start from little things: take the stairs and avoid the escalator or read while standing up instead of lounging on the couch watching tv.

CHAPTER 3

How Your Habits Shape Your Identity

Everybody has bad habits.
You're not the only one with some kind of behavior that might you feel guilty or regretful.

Habits are any repeated behaviors, especially rituals, that we might do on a daily or weekly basis.
Habits come in many different forms.
There are physical habits, like drinking, smoking, or refusing to exercise. Some patterns also lie in the way we behave. Maybe you get in fights with people regularly, or it's easy for you to lash out when you are angry. How you react and interact with individuals can be very convenient in specific ways.

There are a few everyday bad habits that are important to recognize because even though they might seem small, they can lead to more significant issues.
The basal ganglia are where habits are created and stored.

When you continue to cycle through a habit, that formation becomes stronger each time you perform that act.

This is why we improve and get better at things.

If you've never stored information about how to complete a task, each time you did it, would be like the first time.

This small part of the brain can also cause us to repeat things that are bad for us continually, and the more we do it, the harder it is to break.

Breaking Bad Habits and Replacing Them with Good Ones

The first category of habits for you to reflect on is the *coping mechanisms*. This includes stress, eating, drinking or doing any recreational drugs.
On occasion, everybody likes to have a beer at the end of their stressful workday. However, if you're having a beer every single day after work, this isn't as healthy.
Your brain and body are associating that beer with the end of work hours. It's then easier to feel out of place if you go a day without having that post-work beer.
The thing about habits is that on a small scale, they aren't always bad.

As you can see in this example, there's nothing wrong with unwinding with a glass of beer. The problem is when this action becomes repeated, creating a routine on having one or multiple glasses of beer every day after work.

Another bad habit is the way that you view or treat yourself.
For example, every time that you hear good news, you might automatically think it has to be followed by bad news.
Every time you look in the mirror and feel confident, it might be accompanied with the thought about how you are unworthy or not attractive.
Every time somebody compliments you, you might deflect it somewhere else.
If you're not viewing yourself properly, this will impact the ability you have to manage your emotions.

A different bad habit that many individuals commonly have is to put things off.

Is it easier to start your diet on Mondays, right?

It's more common for you to wait until you have the free time to clean out your closet.

You're just too busy right now, right?

The everyday bad habits are so normalized in our society and our lives only because they occur so frequently. Toxic habits can also feel very normal.

For example, you might have grown up in a household where communication was not a very important subject. If somebody had an issue, it might have always led to people lashing out.

Maybe things were thrown, voices were raised, and emotions were high each time there was a minor conflict. This could automatically trigger you to be very combative and defensive, anytime you approach any kind of matter.

This kind of behavior can be constant, but you don't recognize that it's wrong. Since someone was raised with more confrontational parents, it might be standard for you to exhibit that same behavior now.

You don't realize that it's not healthy and that it's actively damaging you, because it's become so normalized.

To quit these habits, you have to identify what they are.

What have you been doing that has negatively impacted your life?

The process of reflection that we've been talking about so far is an essential first step to notice this habit.

It might help you to write down what you are doing in a day and tracking back.

You can also check in with friends or family members and reflect on what unhealthy habits they might have. What do you see other people doing, and is there a way to notice that within yourself?

Often what we emphasize and see in other people is also what we see in ourselves.

For example, if you are very punctual and being on time is crucial to you, you're more likely to identify other people's punctuality because you place that emphasis on yourself first.

If you look at your friends and family and notice they have these bad habits, your behaviors might start coming to the surface, making it easier for you to identify them as they happen.

It is also essential that we replace our bad habits when we do actively try to change them.

Many people fail to switch up their routines and change their habits because they just take them away. They try to stop cold turkey.

It's not an easy task and can make you sink back into the pattern you are trying to break.

Instead of trying to cut yourself off abruptly with old habits, replace them.

Each time you take something away in your daily routine, that's going to create a slot. As you travel throughout your day, you end up falling into that hole unless you replenish that habit with something healthier.

For example, if you have a dessert every single night, that might be an unhealthy habit you want to break. It's not undoubtedly healthy to have many cupcakes, bowls of ice cream, and a slice of cake every single night before you go to bed.

Instead of just trying to quit eating altogether, you need to replace that habit with something else. Have a bowl of fruit, a yoghurt, a smoothie or something else that's healthier, but still sweet to give you that fulfilment to your craving.

If you are going to quit cigarettes, you would want to replace that with another healthy habit as well. You might try chewing gum or even exercise as a way to replenish what is being taken away.

How to Build Better Habits in 5 Simple Steps

Overcoming a habit isn't the easiest thing you'll do, but it is possible when you put the right effort towards it. In order to overcome a habit, there are five things you should do.

The first is to *identify*.
Know what the habit is and why it is terrible that you are consistently doing it.
Try to identify the origin of the habit and trace back to what started it all.

For example, one bad habit might be that you are always picking at your cuticles or biting your nails. Maybe you've only recently started doing this, or perhaps you realize it traced back to your childhood. Why is this bad?

You usually do it when you're feeling anxious and, sometimes it can lead to distraction and overthinking. You might even do it for so long that you end up causing your fingers to bleed.

This identification is necessary for the first step. Admit it out and loud, share with somebody if you want, and write it down.

Giving the acknowledgement and admitting that it is negatively impacting you is the first step towards wanting to make an effort to change.

Confront this habit and be prepared as we move onto step two.

Next, you have to *discover* what your trigger is. Why are you doing this?

What has led to your urge to participate in this cycle? For some, triggers are obvious things, like a craving brought on by watching a commercial.

Other triggers are a little less obvious, such as generalized stress felt at work.

Habits usually develop as an attempt to resolve an issue or find a solution.

For example, if you're picking at your fingers, sometimes it's an attempt to remove yourself from the situation. It gives you something to focus on. It provides an alleviation.

When you can self-groom, it self-soothes.

It makes you feel like you're taking care of yourself. Once you've identified the trigger, you'll be able to either avoid it as needed or be prepared when you might be confronted with it.

The third step is to *find something to replace it* with. As we mentioned previously, you can't just keep taking things away. Your habits are trying to fulfil urges, desires, and alleviate anxieties within you. If you change that habit, you'll be left struggling on your own to confront those issues.

It's best to start with something similar, if possible. For example, wanting to pick at your fingers could be replaced with a fidget gadget, or a hobby you do with your hands like knitting or sewing.

A habit like smoking isn't easily replaced with something similar. There aren't healthy alternatives to smoking, but you could still do something orally, like chewing gum or sucking on a sugar-free lollipop. You can maybe exercise because, with the increase in breathing, you could again feel some similar effects to what the habit of smoking was trying to fulfil. You could get an exercise bike, or even just a jump rope, and decide to do this for five or ten minutes, anyway the long it would have taken you to smoke.

The fourth step is to *reflect* on how well you are doing with the habit.

Check-in with the overall goals you have with yourself and if this new adjustment has helped or hurt you in the process.

What has been working for you? Have you been triggered too frequently?

Is your replacement not working?

For example, if you replaced the urge to pick with a fidget spinner, perhaps this hasn't been doing the job and making you more anxious. You could then try a new method, like getting a manicure to resist the urge to bite your fingernails or a creative hobby like painting to keep your hands busy.

The final step is to *identify and celebrate* the rewards. Notice how life has improved since you removed this habit.

Has it been upgraded with the positive replacement you've been using?

Reward yourself for reiterating further that you have done something to be proud of.

Buy a new outfit, go out to dinner, take a weekend trip if you want!

Whichever method you choose is up to you, but remember you deserve a celebration.

To recap, the steps are:

1. Identify what the **habit** is and why it is bad for you.

2. Notice the **trigger** and urge that you are trying to fulfil.

3. Find the **replacement** to help you stop this habit.

4. Reflect and **adjust** as needed to improve.

5. Find something to **reward** yourself to celebrate your accomplishments.

Use These Learnings to Improve the Quality of Your Future

For the first section, notice everything you can about the habit.

Pick out what the habit is and also when you are likely to do it.

For example, a bad habit is eating candy every night. It's good to identify what that candy might be as well, and a specific time if it occurs regularly. This way, you'll be more knowledgeable about putting your replacement plan into action.

It's also good to note why it is wrong, to give you a more prominent reason to replace it.

The second section is to notice what situations trigger it.

In the example, the trigger is that boredom that comes after dinner but before bed.

After having a big savory dinner, it's easy to want something sweet, especially when you're just relaxing and watching TV.

The third section is identifying what you could replace it with.

If strawberries are your favorite fruit, that's a great snack to use as a replacement because it provides something sweet that you know you'll like.

You can also use Sudoku as a way to keep your mind focused on something instead opting for food; a different activity will help you to calm down a little bit before bed.

The fourth section is to identify any adjustments that you need to make.

What has worked for you so far, and what has not?

In this example, the correction required is that the craving of sweets is still there.

While strawberries provide something sugary, they don't fulfil that deep desire that a caramel candy bar would. In the beginning, you could swap the fruits with dark chocolate, and later on, try to make that habit even healthier.

At first, breaking habits can be hard, so starting smaller is fine.

The last section is a quick reminder of the natural rewards that come along.

It includes anything that will improve based on the changes that you can measure.

For this example, giving up candies has helped you to lose some weight and released more energy to get up in the morning.

You can go out and get ice cream with the family to celebrate healthier habits after thirty days.

While ice cream isn't healthy, it's still a reward for all the other good choices you've made.

Example:

Habit	I am eating caramel candy bars every night at 9:30 P.M.
Trigger	Post-dinner hunger, boredom, cravings for something sweet

Replacement	Strawberries and Sudoku
Adjustments	Dark chocolate instead of strawberries
Reward	More energy in the morning. Five pounds lost in 30 days. Get ice cream with the family as a celebration

Here are a few more practical examples to give you a better sense of how to apply these methods in a different scenario:

Habit	Letting the dishes pile up
Trigger	Not minded doing them, you feel like time is better spent on something else
Replacement	Doing the dishes for twenty minutes every day, listening to a podcast to make the time more enjoyable
Adjustments	Doing the dishes every day is hard, doing them in two phases during the day for 10 minutes is more realistic

Reward	Ordering a delivery meal at the end of the month after consistently doing the dishes

Habit	Playing video games for four hours straight every night
Trigger	Boredom, having nothing else to do
Replacement	One hour of mandated reading for every two hours gaming
Adjustments	No adjustments needed–this has been working great!
Reward	Three hours of videogames on the last Friday night of the month with friends

To help you make the most of these steps, you can use this supplementary chart and fill it with your goals.
Create multiple tables for multiple habits at any time of your life; it doesn't have to be a repetitive cycle with deadlines.

Habit	
Trigger	
Replacement	
Adjustments	
Reward	

CHAPTER 4

Improve a Focused Mind

A healthy mind is a focused mind.
Everybody could use more concentration during day-to-day activities.
We are surrounded by so many inputs that we don't have to worry about a lack of stimulation.
Even the most boring topics can have interesting elements when you look hard enough.
The problem is finding that focus.
Fortunately, we aren't wired to be forever the way we are. Even if it's hard for you to focus on a minute-long video, you can re-train your brain to pay attention.

The left side of your brain controls the right side of your body and vice versa.
For this reason, who had a stroke on the right side of the brain, will see physical effects, like paralysis, on the left side of the body.
The left side is in control of more logical aspects of your brain, while the right is associated with creativity.

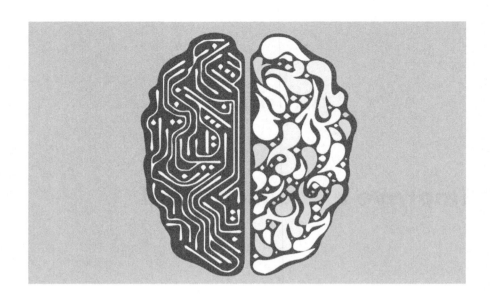

Some experts suggest you can see which side of your brain you are using more by which nostril flares. Sometimes you might find yourself needing to be creative when you are too logical, and maybe in other moments, you can't help but be creative when a more analytical view is suggested.

One good exercise, and one that is helpful to do right now as you continue throughout this book, is a grounding practice to connect both sides of your brain.

Plug your right nostril and breathe in with your left. Breathe out of your right nostril as you plug your left.

You can also do simple things like rubbing your stomach while you are patting your head.
By connecting two actions and stimulating both, you have already taken the necessary steps to control your focus.

Four Principles of Mental Toughness

Four elements show if you are someone who is mentally fit.

These include:

1. Your outlook

2. Your response

3. Your effort

4. Your confidence

Each time you have to focus on something, achieve a goal, or just live life in general, you can check in with these four elements to discover where you might fall on this scale.

The first principle is understanding your life vision.
When it comes to your outlook, how do you view the world?
How do you see the task at hand?
Are you thinking more positively or negatively about the things you have to do?
For example, someone who hates their life might not be as successful as an individual who loves everything about living.

The second principle is how you respond to circumstances.

How do you respond when someone offers constructive criticism?
How do you respond when you fail?
How do you respond when things go unexpected?
Someone who is mentally tough will embrace criticism, learn from their failures, and go with the flow, making adjustments to their plan as needed.
Someone who is mentally unfit will be combative to criticism, let failure keep them from trying again, and experience anxiety when things go wrong.

What effort do you put towards your goals?
How do you cultivate motivation to get things done?
Someone who is mentally fit will be able to self-motivate. They create their purposes and are proactive.
Someone mentally unfit is not going to be able to find their own motivation and instead depend on others to tell them what to do.

Finally, your confidence plays a massive role in how you view yourself and the world around you.
The way you see and criticize yourself reveals a lot about how mentally fit you might be at the moment.

It's OK not to be perfectly "mentally fit."
You might still experience self-doubt or worry, and that's normal and expected.

The imperative thing to remember is that you are checking in with these principles and actively trying to improve them.

The following chart provides an example of differences between mental toughness:

Mental Toughness	LOW	HIGH
Outlook	"I'm unsuccessful, and the world sucks."	"I have made accomplishments and look forward to the future"
Response	"Why even bother? I'll keep failing."	"I have learned from my mistakes, and I will try again!"
Effort	"Who cares, I don't even feel like doing this."	"Even if I fail, I will be confident knowing I did my very best."
Confidence	"I'm a loser."	"I'm a winner."

Improve Concentration

There are a few key factors that, at the moment, might be taking you away from concentration.
The first is biological.
An unhealthy diet, not getting the right amount of sleep, and even being dehydrated, can keep you from focusing. Your brain is all about figuring out what to do for survival.
The first thing your mind wants to make sure is taking care of your basic daily needs.
These needs include rest, hydration, and nutrition. If you lack on those, your concentration is not going to be able to focus on anything else.
You have to make sure these requirements are being met.
Just because you have eaten doesn't mean that you have provided your body with nutrition, either. Often concentration can waiver because you might still be hungry, or you are not getting those minimum nutritional elements satisfied right from the start.
Make sure that you check in with your nutrition and follow the previous steps that we have laid out for choosing a healthier diet.

Once your biology is all set, and you've taken care of everything - including your hunger, your tiredness, and all other chemical factors - you then have to identify behaviors that keep you from concentrating.
These are seemingly small habits, such as checking your phone frequently.
If you are planning to sit and watch a 90-minute movie, you might not be able to be focused the whole time without checking your phone.

Identify and remove these behavioral habits that are affecting your concentration just like you would with biological factors, as we have discussed previously in this book.

However, after everything's been taken care of, sometimes it's still just hard to focus. But don't give up.

Identify the subject matter and the reason why it might be difficult for you to be concentrated.

If there is an external factor, such as loud noises outside or a chatty roommate, you might have to remove yourself from the situation and find a different setting that makes it easier to focus.

The other problem might be that the subject material is simply not interesting to you.

It is easier to daydream about fantasy scenarios and other fun things rather than paying attention to the snooze fest in front of you.

Once you've picked out the reason why it is hard for you to concentrate, then you can find the solution.

If the subject material is simply boring for you to focus on, then it is time to find a way to make it more interesting.

For example, you might sing a song to help you better remember the material that you're studying.

You could watch a documentary or a movie about a subject that you're studying.

You can find different learning resources on the internet, whether it is through YouTube videos, or even reaching out to friends and family on social media.

You can also find a way to make the subject material more enjoyable by simply playing music, or maybe changing your setting scenario.

For example, staying in a stuffy room and read 60 pages of history material might be more interesting if you could do it in the park.

You might even play some atmosphere music to make your reading a bit more stimulating.

Make sure you sit up straight and don't put yourself in a place where it is easy to fall asleep.

Create a very focused setting.

If you are trying to study in bed, your brain is going to tell you that this is the place where you go to sleep; the task will become more tiring, and your mind will try to convince you to fall asleep.

If you read a book where usually sitting to watch the TV, or where you typically eat snacks, your brain will tell you that it is time to turn on the TV and eat some snacks.

You have to create an intentionally focused space to be more mentally aware in that setting.

If you choose your desk to be your focus space, as soon as you sit down at that desk, your brain is going to snap into concentration mode.

Make sure that you get rid of the clutter as well. If you have a stack of unread books sitting in the corner, that is just going to stress you out and remind your brain of all the things that you still have to do.

The most important thing about concentration is making sure that you give yourself breaks.

Never go more than 90 minutes of reading, studying, writing, or doing anything else mental. You have to physically remove yourself from the situation and context, stimulate your brain in another way, and then go back to your work.

Sometimes you might just not be able to focus on your work. That's fine. If things are not working, and you simply cannot concentrate, try to do something else, and go back to it later.

The thing is, most of us don't want to do that; we want just to get the work done and get it over.
Maybe you have to clean your house later, but you'd instead just work now because cleaning is more fun to you than what you have to get done.
However, you might end up procrastinating all day, not getting anything done, and then you have to work and clean.

Try to switch different tasks around so that you can give your concentration to the things that need it the most.

Learn to Optimize and Maximize Results

As you begin to improve your focus, the progression is to increase your productivity.
To make the most out of the least amount of time possible, you have a few important principles to remember.

The first thing to do is to make sure that you are planning your day right.
Primary, prioritize your tasks.
What needs to get done on the simplest level?
Categorize these tasks as well. Section them off into things that take a long time, and something that you can get done quickly.

Categorize or label them by activities that are going to be very challenging and things that you do very straightforwardly. You can also organize them by the things that you are excited to do and the things that you do not want to do.

Then create a blank template of your schedule. Identify and label your time slots as well. At what point are you the most productive? When are you the least productive? When do you have the freedom to be flexible with your schedule and when do you need to stick to something a little stricter?

For example, Monday mornings, you might know that you are absolutely not productive. You don't feel like doing anything; you'd instead just catch up with the news and postpone the not urgent tasks for the next day. Wednesdays might be very free for you. You have nothing to do after work so, if things ran over a little bit, you could take the time. You know Thursdays you are incredibly productive; you are excited for the weekend. You don't have much work left to do and, it is easy for you to breeze through even the most challenging task. Friday, maybe you have a dinner appointment at 6:30 sharp, so you can't under any circumstance, work past 5 p.m.

Label and identify your days and, then, you can easily match up your tasks with those times.

The tasks that you do not want to do might be best saved for Thursday when you're in a good mood and, you have that motivation.

Duties that are easy and mindless you can do Monday mornings when you're not that motivated.

Things that might take you a little more time than you expect could be scheduled for Wednesday, and tasks that you know will be able to be completed more quickly can be saved for Friday.

Of course, your schedule might not look anything like this, but it's an example of how you can prioritize and rearrange things to make the most of your time.

Another essential principle to remember is to chunk the time together.

Are you able to perform more than one task, or activity, at the same time? Now, this doesn't mean to fall into the trap of multitasking.

Often, we end up giving 50% of our focus to each thing, rather than giving it 100% to both.

Multitasking should only be done with things that require different parts of your body.

For example, watching a documentary and cleaning out your closet can be done simultaneously.

Watching a documentary and trying to write a paper should not be done together, just as you wouldn't try to clean the closet and do the dishes at the same time.

Mindless tasks - like cleaning - can be paired with mindful tasks - like listening. -

The most important fact to remember above all is not letting yourself the stress and worry about wasted time. Time might have slipped away from you, and maybe a task you hoped to get done in 30 minutes has taken over four hours.

Of course, those feelings are going to be distracting, and it is not as simple to change as saying, "*don't worry.*"

You might have regret that you should have done something sooner and feel anger or frustration at yourself for not trying hard enough. You have to let go of that stress and keep focused on moving forward. You might have already wasted time, but you are going to allow even more slip away from you if you keep ruminating on those negative emotions.

To overcome this fear, you can get to the root of what it is stressing you out.

You might be sitting there thinking, *"Oh my gosh, I'm wasting so much time. What am I doing with my time? What's wrong with me? Why I can't do this?"*

However, ask yourself, *"What would I be doing better with my time? What am I truly missing out that causes me such stress?"*

Sometimes the stress of just wasting time makes us feel panicked.

However, lost time isn't always wrong if you are still learning something or doing something productive in that time.

While it might have taken you three hours extra to complete a task, you still managed to get that task done, and you probably did it more effectively than if you were to rush it.

Embrace each moment and find something valuable from it.

Even if you spent five hours scrolling on your phone, there were probably a few things that you learned. Maybe you read an interesting article, a friend shared an inspirational tip, or you simply learned some exciting news you weren't aware of before.

Rather than trying to make more time, be aware of how you are using that time, and make each moment profitable to shape and develop your mentality.

64

Control and Avoid Distractions

Distractions are hard to avoid. You want to remove as many distractions from your life, such as watching TV while you try to work, chatting with friends, or having your phone right next to you beeping and buzzing every time you want to do something.
There are many apparent distractions, and you are likely already aware of what these are.
Remove these distractions as best as you can, but also be aware of more hidden distractions that might be pulling you from where you should be focusing.

For example, our thoughts can be very distracting. You might be thinking about all that you are missing out on; maybe you are also stressed or worried about what you are going to be doing later on.

Wondering if somebody is mad at you, being stressed about how others perceive you, and being constantly worried about what people are thinking can all be very distracting.

In the next chapter, we will go over those negative emotions and how you can rework them but for now, just remind yourself that even your own thoughts could be the very thing keeping you distracted.
The best way to avoid physical distractions is to identify them before they come.
Let's say that you're planning to do research online all night. Your biggest distraction is going to be the accessibility of your browser; you might see other interesting articles on the pages that you are searching on while you do study. Maybe it's habitual for you to check in with social media each time you open a new tab.
To avoid a distraction like this, you can put blockers on your phone or computer through different apps to prevent you from access on your social media pages.
If you are going to do a group task at a colleague' house, you may identify that his/her roommate is a distraction; maybe, instead of meeting at the colleague' house, you could meet in a co-working space.
If you're planning on reading at home later in the day, your kids might be a distraction or even just too needy. Before you even confront these distractions, come up with your game plan to overcome them. You could put on a movie for the kids or take your dog for a walk and tire them out, so they go to sleep when you get home.

Procrastination, in general, can be very toxic and keep us from getting the things that we want.

First, identify why we procrastinate. One of the top reasons is because we are afraid of failure.

If you push off finishing a paper for school, it feels better because then you don't have to worry about getting that bad grade.

If you procrastinate working out, then you don't have to feel bad about not achieving results.

There could be a more significant reason why you are not focusing.

Procrastination also comes merely because we are not very interested in the task that we have to complete.

To avoid procrastination, make sure that you sit yourself down where you need to complete a task and taking the first step.

If you have to study, sit at your desk and at least open up your computer. It sounds so easy but getting started is always the hardest part. Once you sit there with the laptop open, it is easy to get into the flow of studying.

Let's say that you're sitting in the living room on your phone, talking to your roommate, watching TV, and just relaxing.

You have to start studying, or else you are going to fall behind.

However, you have to go to your room to study because you know that your roommate is going to be hanging out all night.

Your option is to clean off your desk and sit in front of the computer to study, but it gives you an overwhelming feeling.

Right now, in this situation, the starting point is getting up off of the couch.

However, take things a little bit slower.

Use visualization to picture yourself completing the task.

Close your eyes and envision yourself standing up and walking to your room.

Picture going through the motions of sitting down and opening your computer.

Sometimes our brain hasn't precisely registered what it needs to do next, so using visualization can help implant that motivation naturally.

To accomplish the task, start by setting up your desk. Then, if you want, you can go back into the living room and take another 10-minute break.

Then go back and sit at your desk and open up your computer.

Sit there on your phone still if you have to for a few minutes. Sometimes the pressure of starting is too much, so it is better to ease into it.

Rather than thinking that you have to dive right into the icy cold pool and waiting for the right motivation, allow yourself to walk in slowly. It might only take you two hours to prepare and finish a task, but you might also take three hours even to start!

You may be intended to start studying at eight o'clock, now it is 8:30, and you are still sitting there on your phone. Rather than saying, *"I have to start right away at 8:45"*, instead give yourself until 10:00. In the meantime, go set up your room; open your computer, and get comfortable with that study space. You will likely to start even earlier than 10:00, but by giving yourself that room to breathe, it keeps you from feeling like you are suffocating.

Make sure that you are only doing things in small portions.

If you have a 10-page paper to write, don't expect yourself to sit down and write ten pages in one go. Write three pages for a start, then do something like making dinner or doing the dishes. Go back and write three more pages. Then, take a shower or eat a snack. Write the last four pages, and so on.

Having somebody hold you accountable is also very helpful. You can share your goal with somebody else, and they can make sure that you are sticking to it and getting things done in the most efficient way possible.

Once you start to identify the reasons that you are procrastinating, it is easier to overcome them and get your work done.

CHAPTER 5

How to Control Your Feelings and Emotions

Before going over some negative emotions or thought processes you are having, it is central to recognize the difference between negative and bad.

Everybody has negative feelings. That doesn't mean that you are broken, that you are a terrible person, or that there is something wrong with you.

The point to identify is that these negative emotions or mental patterns end up leaving you in a cynical space. They make you believe the world is a bad place or that you are a wrong person; they give you the perspective that everything is negative rather than just your thoughts.

When we say negative emotions, we are not trying to make you feel bad or like you should be ashamed. Instead, we want you to recognize how these patterns of thinking are keeping you trapped in an adverse space and can prevent you from thriving, really diminishing your ability to have self-control.

Negative emotions are often brought on by cognitive distortions.

Dealing with Negative Emotions

Any cognitive distortion is a cycle of thought that keeps you trapped in the same way of thinking over and over again.
To have self-control, you need to have a positive outlook on life. You have to feel motivated and proud of yourself. Positivity is not all about being ignorantly happy. It's not obliviousness or complete bliss, because you're still able to recognize the wrong things.

Changing these thought processes around and preventing them from taking over your ability to think is only going to help you improve.

One of the most common negative patterns of thinking is believing that everything is black or white. Change the idea that everything is good or bad, all or nothing. Black and white thought often makes you use absolute phrases and words as well, like 'best,' or 'worst,' 'always,' or 'never.'

For example, let's say you have a friend who had a pretty decent day. This person woke up, went to work on time, getting things done, came home, and everything went as expected. However, he/she got a letter in the mail saying that they are past due on one of their bills. Maybe he/she get upset, throw their mail across the room and say, "This is the worst day ever." Of course, a bad thing happened that day. But your friend doesn't have to label the entire day just because of that singular moment.

Often people let five minutes of their time dictate five hours or longer!
It's easy to let these thoughts get out of control because often our brains work from one moment to the next. We make associations and connections in our mind to help us have a better understanding of the world around us.
Unfortunately, this can let you stay in a very polarized place where you do not correctly recognize reality.
You must recognize the grey areas of your thoughts, and deal with the negative emotions that are coming from them.
Have a spectrum in your mind and pay attention to both the good and the bad.
For each bad experience you have, there is likely a positive one to go along with it.
If you genuinely cannot find the good in a situation that is just a signal that things need to change.

When you think you are not enough and you don't have any evidence to combat that, it doesn't mean that you necessarily are, but it is a signal that maybe there is a higher chance that needs to be made within yourself.

Negative emotions often come when we jump to conclusions.

Making any sort of assumptions or trying to fill in the blanks on your own can leave you feeling, sad and disappointed.

Talking about sentimentalism, it might happen in life that somebody you have a crush on isn't texting you back. It's been two hours, and they haven't responded. They usually respond within 20 minutes, so this has you worried.

It's easy to jump to the conclusion that they hate you. Maybe they don't like you, and they're never going to text you back again.

Maybe they are sleeping with somebody else at this very moment.

Perhaps they took a screenshot of your text and sent it to all their friends and now every single person they know is laughing at you.

Anyone of us could jump to these dire conclusions, but often the assumptions we make are from our negative thoughts than from reality.

Have you considered if the person you are texting is just in the shower and haven't seen the message?

What about if this person is nervous about texting you back as you are waiting for his/her response.

Again, you need to balance these thoughts when you deal with these emotions.

One helpful tip is to always talk to yourself in the way you would speak to a friend.

If you had your beloved friend come to you with anxiety, what would you try to tell them to alleviate those emotions?

That is the way how we have to talk to ourselves.

It is easy to cast blame inwards. Maybe you punish yourself and torment your mentality by replaying the negative things you have done in your past, keeping you locked up in your lethal mental prison.

It is easy to feel negative emotions when we practice personalization; by this process, we are assuming that everything involves us. Personalization can often happen because of we are very insecure about ourselves.

Does it ever occur you hear a group of people snickered in the corner when you were out at the mall? You might have assumed they were making fun of you for your clothes or the way you were walking.

Again, find that balance.

What would you tell a friend who believed in that scenario? You would say that a group of friends is probably laughing at something that happened to them. Maybe you'd explain, *"Even if they were laughing at you, who cares? Do you care about the opinion of somebody who makes that un of strangers?"*

It's easy to help a friend out, so why is it so hard to do the same for yourself?

Blaming is also a very toxic pattern that can cause negative emotions.

Remember that nobody else is responsible for the way that you feel. They might influence certain factors and thoughts inside of you, but at the end of the day, you are the one who is in control of your emotions.

Casting blame onto other people is not going to help you.

When you blame somebody, you are giving them power. Not only are you giving them control over the situation, but they also now have free rein of your emotions.

By imputing somebody for your bad mood, you might even be giving them the power to change that into a good mood.

However, it is always you who is responsible for altering these emotions.

Get to the root of those issues to confront these negative feelings.

What is it that makes you so afraid of who you are?

That insecurity can drive you to act out in specific ways, and that often will influence your patterns of thoughts.

Make Decisions Before the Negative Emotions Take Over You

Having self-control isn't just about saying 'no' to impulses. It is also about saying 'yes' to sometimes tricky decisions that might have you shredded.
It can be challenging to agree to certain things or say 'yes' instantly because you are afraid of the results. One thing to remember above all is that not take a decision is always going to be the worst choice that you can make.
Overthinking is easy to do.
You might feel confident and have all the knowledge necessary to agree to a situation; but then the doubt comes, and you start to be thinking "*Well, what if I did this?*" or "*What if that happens?*"

Of course, the *what-ifs* are always going to be there. You have to remember when making decisions and confronting your emotions; you are still going to be able to question things.
There will always be gray areas that you could dive deeper into; that is what life is all about.
There is no singular viewpoint. There is no clear right or wrong.
Quitting a job without giving notice might seem as absolutely forbidden to some people. You just don't do it — it is irresponsible.
However, what if you were offered your dream job and needed to start tomorrow?
What if your current employer was verbally abusing you, and you somehow found the strength to get out?
What if you finally found the courage to turn your dream hobby into a career reality?

All of these underlying reasons are gray areas depending on a variety of factors, like cultural background, religion, past experiences, current situations, mental health, and general morals.

Indecision doesn't occur exclusively with life-changing events; it happens even with small things.
Choosing what kind of cereal to buy at the grocery store might leave you standing in the aisle for 20 minutes.
Indecision often happens because of our lack of self-direction and constant self-doubt.
To overcome this, you have to give yourself time limits. Cut yourself off after a certain amount of thought.

You can dive into these deep layers and holes of the decisions you have to make, but at some point, you have to set that boundary within yourself.
Identify why it is so hard for you to make decisions. For some people, are things like which grocery store to go. A more significant issue is picking a life partner. Maybe you go on first dates over and over and over again, but you never make it to that second one because it is too hard for you to commit to anybody.

The problem often isn't the lack of choices, but instead something inside of ourselves that is telling us that every decision we make is wrong.
This idea is mostly coming from insecurity and frequently because we do not have that control. Especially in our wide-open world that we have now, choices are going to feel unlimited.

A hundred years ago, you normally had to find a spouse in the geographical location where you lived. Now you can fall in love with somebody half-way across the world.
The decisions are always going to be there, and you have unlimited choices; now, it is about using your self-control to limit yourself.

One thing you have to remember is to address regret and guilt. Usually, the more remorse that a person feels, the harder it is to make a decision.
If you are constantly regretful and always hating every decision you have made in your life, then likely it is hard for you to do small things. You might regret where you have moved, what you studied in college, or even who you married.
A regretful mind like that can leave you doubtful in the future.

It might even be the reason why it is hard for you to pick a certain kind of cheese when you are at the supermarket.

Manage regret and guilt by recognizing that they are not useful. These are unproductive patterns of thought, and instead, you should find something valuable from these experiences, and then move on.

You might feel guilty about a situation.

First, identify what you can do to make sure that you don't endure that situation again.

Every time that you find yourself travelling back into that mindset and wanting to go over it again, distract yourself.

Practice mindfulness.

Meditate.

Go for a walk and remove yourself from that thought process, because it is only going to hurt you.

Remind yourself that even the bad things that you have lived through have been influential in developing the person that you are today.

A lot of the valuable lessons that we learn from life come from negative experiences.

Most of the hardest issues that we have ever faced turned into what makes us the strong individuals that we are today.

Yes, you might make the wrong decision again.

You might choose the worst item on the menu at a restaurant.

You might end up committing yourself to a six-month relationship to somebody who isn't right for you.

You go through these experiences, and you can still learn something from them, even when they don't have the outcome that you desired.

Instead of thinking about the situation or thinking about the what-ifs, think about completing and finishing things now. Make that decision!

Make that choice and stop second-guessing every last thing that you would do.
Listen to the advice that you would give to a friend.
What would be your suggestion?
Open your mind to all possible solutions. Sometimes decisions are more than the two-sided of a coin, so for that, you can also roll the dice.
Get a piece of paper and label your choices and give them a number from one to six.
Roll the dice and go with it.
Whatever you do, just do something, because afterwards is what matters the most.

We can never be ready for all things that are going to occur. Even situations that you think you have correctly prepared are likely going to be disrupted by some factor.
Nothing ever happens the way we planned to be, and you shouldn't want it to be.
Life is all about those exciting little elements of surprise that you would never have been able to predict from the start.

Embrace that uncertainty and let that be a powerful tool to help you make better decisions and maintain a healthy level of self-control.

Conclusion

The process of changing your mindset is long, and you can't overlook the physical and practical actions you have to do along the way.
Staring outside of the window and reflecting about life seems dramatic to some, but it can be a helpful tool to bring you closer to yourself.
However, it is not the only thing you can do.
Creating a steady fitness routine, eating more natural foods, and managing your stress are all things that can actively bring you closer to achieving your goals, no matter how unrelated they might be.

Remind yourself that at the end of the day self-love always wins!

Berating, bullying, and belittling yourself is not going to help you to improve your quality life. Conversely, it can weaken your confidence and lead to a greater desire to give in to impulses.
Remark the thoughts you need to change and become more aware of unhealthy patterns is the first important step.

Moving forward, you have to train your brain continuously.
It is like going to the gym and expect to walk out with a new body after the very first work out.
When it comes to getting strong mentally, it is required the same dedication and patience.

Don't forget that overdoing can be as just as damaging. You need breaks and even dull moments of activity.
Whether it is a videogame or a reality TV show, give yourself this mental "junk food", because we all need a pause from time to time.

Finding your balance is recognizing the healthy pressures you feel when you challenge yourself in a progression; it is the acceptance to pull back yourself when you have pushed a little too hard.
Always prioritize yourself.
While it might feel selfish, doesn't make you believe you are better than anyone else.

Think in this way: is like the flight announcement about the safety instruction to put your oxygen mask on before you help another person to put it on. If you did this the opposite way around, you would suffocate before you got the chance to place your mask.

You can't fill someone else's basket if yours is empty!

Visualize yourself in the future and nourish not just who you are today, but the person that you are going to become.
To see everlasting results, feed into the life vision you have created and frequently check-in with yourself to question your values, motivations, and practices.
Be honest with yourself because it is you who will hurt the most through personal dishonesty.

The point of life is to have fun, thrive and be the best you can at all times.
Chasing happiness is fruitless because nothing is waiting for you at the end.
All of the greatness available is already surrounding you.

Embrace now this new start.

References

Armstrong, B. (2018). How Exercise Affects Your Brain. Retrieved from https://www.scientificamerican.com/article/how-exercise-affects-your-brain/

Collins, R. (2017). Top 10 Ways to Avoid Procrastination. Retrieved from https://www.collegexpress.com/articles-and-advice/majors-and-academics/blog/top-10-ways-avoid-procrastination/

Daskal, L. (n.d.). 10 Smart Tips to Prevent Distractions and Sharpen Your Focus. Retrieved from https://www.inc.com/lolly-daskal/10-smart-tips-to-prevent-distractions-and-sharpen-your-focus.html

Edberg, H. (2020). How to Stop Overthinking Everything: 12 Simple Habits. Retrieved from https://www.positivityblog.com/how-to-stop-overthinking/

Grohol, J. (2019). 15 Common Cognitive Distortions. Retrieved from https://psychcentral.com/lib/15-common-cognitive-distortions/
Heshmat, S. (2017). 10 Strategies for Developing Self-Control. Retrieved from https://www.psychologytoday.com/us/blog/science-choice/201703/10-strategies-developing-self-control

Knapton, S. (2018). Exercising for 90 Minutes or More Could Make Mental Health Worse, Study Suggests. Retrieved from https://www.telegraph.co.uk/science/2018/08/08/exercising-90-minutes-could-make-mental-health-worse-study-suggests/

Maloney, D. (2020). Keep Your Day in Check: Build Productive Work Habits in 5 Steps. Retrieved from https://slackhq.com/build-productive-work-habits

McCartney, M. (206). How to Do the Most Work in the Shortest Time. Retrieved from https://www.theguardian.com/commentisfree/2016/jun/06/how-to-do-most-work-shortest-time

McQuillan, S. (2019). 9 Ways to Practice Self-Control and Improve Your Life. Retrieved from https://www.psychologytoday.com/us/blog/cravings/201905/9-ways-practice-self-control-and-improve-your-life

Raypole, C. (2019). 12 Tips to Improve Your Concentration. Retrieved from https://www.healthline.com/health/mental-health/how-to-improve-concentration

Schuhmacher, L. (2015). Stress Reduces Self-Control. Retrieved from https://science.sciencemag.org/content/349/6252/1067.3

Whickman, F. (2012). Your Brain's Technical Specs. Retrieved from https://slate.com/technology/2012/04/north-koreas-2-mb-of-knowledge-taunt-how-many-megabytes-does-the-human-brain-hold.html

Printed in Great Britain
by Amazon

37675798R00056